Space

Written by Janine Amos
Reading consultants: Christopher Collier and Alan Howe,
Bath Spa University, UK

First published by Parragon in 2008
Parragon
Queen Street House
4 Queen Street
Bath BA1 1HE, UK

ISBN 978-1-4075-1839-8

Printed in China

space
shuttle

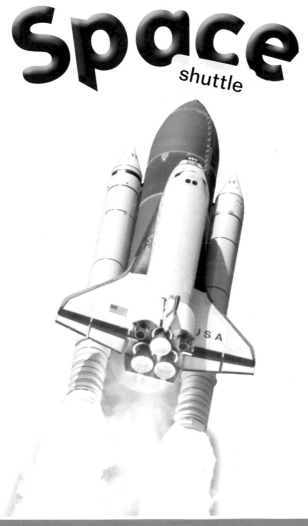

Bath New York Singapore Hong Kong Cologne Delhi Melbourne

Parents' notes

This book is part of a series of non-fiction books designed to appeal to children learning to read.

Each book has been developed with the help of educational experts.

At the end of each book is a quiz to help your child remember the information and the meanings of some of the words and sentences. There is also a glossary of difficult words relating to the subject matter in the book, and an index.

Contents

6   Night sky

8   Our star

10   The planets

12   Other space objects

14   Our solar system

16   Looking into space

18   Famous astronomers

20   Astronauts in space

22   Space station

24   Space probes

26   Quiz

28   Glossary

30   Index

galaxy

Night sky

When you look at the night sky you can see thousands of stars. They are so far away that they look tiny. But really they are giant balls of glowing gas.

Our Sun is a star.

All the stars we can see are part of our galaxy. A galaxy is a massive group of stars.

The temperature at the heart of a star reaches around 29 million degrees Fahrenheit.

The universe is made up of everything in time and space. It is growing all the time.

There are a lot of galaxies in the universe. Our galaxy is called the Milky Way.

Our star

Our star is called the Sun. Earth and the other planets travel around the Sun.

The Sun is our closest star. It is more than a million times bigger than Earth.

The planets travel around the Sun along a path called an orbit. As they go, they spin around and around like tops. They are kept in their orbit by a force called gravity.

Earth orbits the Sun. It takes about 365 days, or one year.

The Moon orbits Earth. This takes about one month.

The planets

All the planets that orbit the Sun are different. On some the air is poisonous. Others are burning hot or freezing cold or covered in dust.

Mercury

Venus

Earth

Mars

Jupiter

Sun

The planets closest to the Sun are called inner planets. They are made mainly of rock and metal. Earth is one of them.

The planets farthest from the Sun are called outer planets. They are huge balls made mainly of gas.

Saturn

Uranus

Neptune

Other space objects

Have you ever seen a shooting star streaking across the night sky? Space is not completely empty. There is dust, gas, rock, and ice whizzing about at high speed.

Asteroids are massive space rocks. Most move around the Sun in a band called the asteroid belt.

This picture shows a huge crater in Arizona. It was made by a meteor crashing into Earth.

DiscoveryFact™

Every year, thousands of pieces of space rock fall onto Earth. Most fall into the ocean.

Comets are balls of ice with long, shining tails of dust and gas.

Meteors are made of burning space dust. We know them as "shooting stars."

Our solar system

The planets and their moons are part of our solar system. So is everything else that travels around the Sun, from the largest asteroid to the smallest speck of dust.

Sun

Mercury

Earth

Saturn

Uranus

DiscoveryFact™

Our solar system also contains at least four dwarf planets. Eris is the biggest dwarf planet.

Venus

Mars

Jupiter

Neptune

Looking into space

For hundreds of years people have used telescopes to look into space. Telescopes make faraway objects look closer.

observatory

DiscoveryFact™

In 1957, a Russian dog named Laika was the first animal to be sent into space.

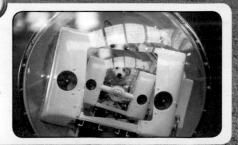

Yuri Gagarin

Neptune   comet   asteroid

satellite dish   crater

probe   Voyager

Galileo Galilei   Stephen Hawking   meteor

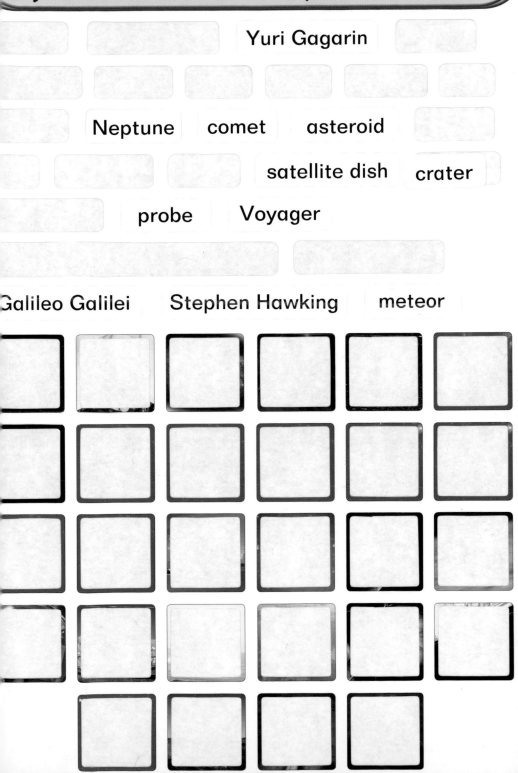

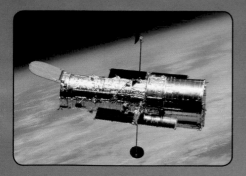

Big telescopes are kept in buildings called observatories. Most observatories are built on high land away from city lights.

A satellite dish collects radio waves given off by objects in space. In New Mexico, 27 dishes work together.

Earth's atmosphere stops us from seeing some stars and planets. The Hubble Space Telescope orbits beyond the atmosphere so it can see more clearly into space.

Very Large Array, New Mexico

satellite

Famous astronomers

People have been studying the universe for thousands of years. People who study space are called astronomers.

Galileo Galilei (1564–1642) was one of the first people to use a telescope to study the sky. He learned that the planets move around the Sun.

DiscoveryFact™

Stephen Hawking is studying the sky today. He believes that humans must find new homes on other planets.

Isaac Newton (1643–1727) figured out why the planets move around the Sun. He learned that a force called gravity keeps them circling there.

Johannes Kepler (1571–1630) used mathematics to figure out how the planets move.

William Herschel (1738–1822) built a huge telescope. His sister was also an astronomer.

Astronauts in space

Hundreds of people have traveled into space. Maybe one day you might travel into space, too. astronaut

Yuri Gagarin was the first person in space. He was a Russian cosmonaut. He traveled once around Earth.

Neil Armstrong, an American astronaut, was the first person to walk on the Moon. His footprint is still there. There is no rain and no wind to blow it away.

Today, the Space Shuttle is launched by booster rockets. In less than 10 minutes, it reaches space.

Space station

A space station is a huge workplace in space. People carry out experiments there, and collect information about the stars and planets.

The International Space Station

International Space Station

When astronauts work outside, they wear a special suit to protect them. They carry a backpack with air to breathe.

Crew members attach their sleeping bags to the station's walls for a good night's sleep.

There is microgravity in space. It makes you feel as if you are floating.

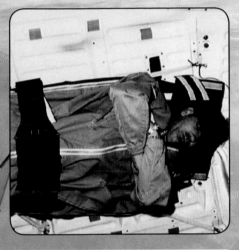

Objects will float about, too. Everything is strapped down—even meal trays.

Space probes

Robot probes explore places people cannot reach, and send information back to Earth.

Voyagers I and *II* are traveling in deep space. They are carrying friendly messages in case they are found by aliens.

Two-thirds of probes sent to Mars have not completed their missions. It's called the Mars Curse!

The probe *Galileo* traveled around Jupiter 34 times. It sent pictures and information back to Earth.

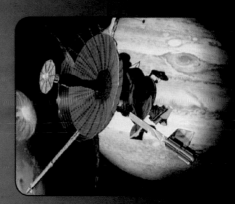

The *Cassini-Huygens* spacecraft reached Saturn and its moons in 2004. The Huygens probe can collect far more information than a human space explorer.

Quiz

Now try this quiz!
All the answers can be found in this book.

What is the name of our galaxy?

(a) The Donut
(b) The Chocolate Cake
(c) The Milky Way

Which was the first animal to be
sent into space Laika

(a) A dog
(b) A cat
(c) A horse

Where do you put your sleeping bag
in a space station?

(a) In a tent
(b) On the floor
(c) On the wall

How many days does it take Earth
to orbit the Sun?

(a) About 3 days
(b) About 36 days
(c) About 365 days

What is a comet made of?

(a) Ice
(b) Wood
(c) Potatoes

Who was the first person to travel into space?

(a) Neil Armstrong
(b) Yuri Gagarin
(c) Galileo Galilei

Glossary

Astronaut A person who is trained to travel in space.

Atmosphere The invisible cloak of air that surrounds Earth. It is made up of gas, water, and dust.

Cosmonaut A Russian astronaut.

Galaxy A large group of billions of stars.

Gravity The force that holds us to the ground and keeps Earth in orbit around the Sun.

Microgravity A state of low gravity, where astronauts and objects in a space station appear to float.

Planet A large ball of rock or gas that travels around a star.

Probe

A spacecraft with no crew that explores in space and sends information back to Earth.

Satellite

An object that travels around a planet. A natural satellite is also called a moon. An artificial satellite has been made by humans.

Solar system

The group of planets, comets, and asteroids that move around the Sun.

Space

Everything beyond Earth's atmosphere.

Index

a

air 10, 21, 22
aliens 24
animals in space 16
Armstrong, Neil 21
asteroid belt 12
asteroids 12, 14
astronauts 20, 21, 22, 23
astronomers 18-19
atmosphere 17

c

Cassini-Huygens
spacecraft 25
comets 13
cosmonauts 20
craters 12

d

dust 10, 12, 13, 14
dwarf planets 15

e

Earth 8, 9, 10, 11, 12, 13,
   14, 17, 20
Eris 15

g

Gagarin, Yuri 20
galaxies 6, 7

Galileo Galilei 18
Galileo space probe 25
gas 6, 11, 12, 13
gas giants 11
gravity 9, 19

h

Hawking, Stephen 19
Herschel, William 19
Hubble Space Telescope
17

i

ice 12, 13
inner and outer planets 11

j

Jupiter 10, 15, 25

k

Kepler, Johannes 19

m

Mars 10, 15, 25
Mercury 10, 14
metals 11
meteors 12, 13
microgravity 23
Milky Way 7
Moon 9, 21

moons 14, 25

n
Neptune 11, 15
Newton, Isaac 19
night sky 6, 12

o
observatories 17
orbit 9, 10

p
planets 8, 9, 10-11, 14, 15,
    17, 18, 19, 22

r
radio waves 17
rings 11
rocks 11, 12, 13

s
satellite dishes 17
satellites 17
Saturn 11, 14, 25
shooting stars 12, 13
solar system 14-15
sound 21
space probes 24-25
Space Shuttle 21
space stations 22-23

space travel 20-21
stars 6, 7, 8, 17, 22
Sun 6, 8-9, 10, 12, 14,
    18, 19

t
telescopes 16-17, 18, 19
temperatures 7

u
universe 7, 18
Uranus 11, 14

v
Venus 10, 15
Voyagers I and *II* 24

Acknowledgements

t=top, c=center, b=bottom, r=right, l=left

Cover: NASA/Roger Ressmeyer/Corbis

p 5tl Reuters/Corbis, p 6ml Denis Scott/Corbis, p 6-7 Alessandro
Della Bella/epa/Corbis, p 8-9 Denis Scott/Corbis, p 9tr Farhad
Parsa/zefa/Corbis, p 9br Denis Scott/Corbis, p 10 Tim Kiusalaas/
Corbis , p 11 Tim Kiusalaas/Corbis, p 12-13 Bryan Allen/Corbis, p
12mr NASA/JPL, p 13tr Denis Scott/CorbisJames, p 13ml Roger
Ressmeyer/Corbis, p 13mr Reuters/Corbis, p 14-15 Denis Scott/
Corbis, p 14 -15 Tim Kiusalaas/Corbis, p 16-17 Mark Chivers/
Robert Harding World Imagery/Corbis, p 17tl NASA, p 17b Richard
T. Nowitz/Corbis, p 16br Marc Garanger/Corbis, p 18l Bettmann/
Corbis, p 19tr The Gallery Collection/Corbis, p 19ml Rune Hellestad/
Corbis, p 19bl Bettmann/Corbis, p 19br Bettmann/Corbis, p 20-21
Corbis, p 20l Bettmann/Corbis, p 20r Stocktrek/Corbis, p 21bl Nasa,
p 22m NASA via CNP, p 23tl NASA, p 23tr NASA, p 23bl nasa, p 23
br NASA, p 24-25 Time & Life Pictures/Getty Image, p 25tr NASA,
p 25mr NASA/JSC, p 25br epa/Corbis, p 27m NASA/JPL, p 27b
Denis Scott/Corbis, p 28-31 Bryan Allen/Corbis